MY FIRST ACTIVITY BOOK

Let's Learn WORD FAMILIES

READ + WRITE

RHYMING WORDS

BLUE APPLE

Art by Yukiko Kido

pig

p i g

p**ig** in a w**ig**

__**ig** in a __**ig**

d**ig**

d _ _ g

pig digs in a wig

__ig __igs in a __ig

jig

j_ _

Put a **pig** in the **wig**.

hug

h_u_g

hug on a rug

__ug on a __ug

b**ug**

b_ _ _

bugs on a **rug**

Can you draw a rug?

__ **ug**s on a __ **ug**

m**ug**

m＿＿＿

b**ug**s on a m**ug**
on a r**ug**

Draw a mug.
Then draw bugs.

___**ug**s on a ___**ug** on a ___**ug**

Draw a **big** b**ug**!

bat

b a t

hat

h _ _

__ at

___ ___ ___

__ at

___ ___ ___

__ at

___ ___ ___

__ at

___ ___ ___

Draw a **bat** on a **rug**.

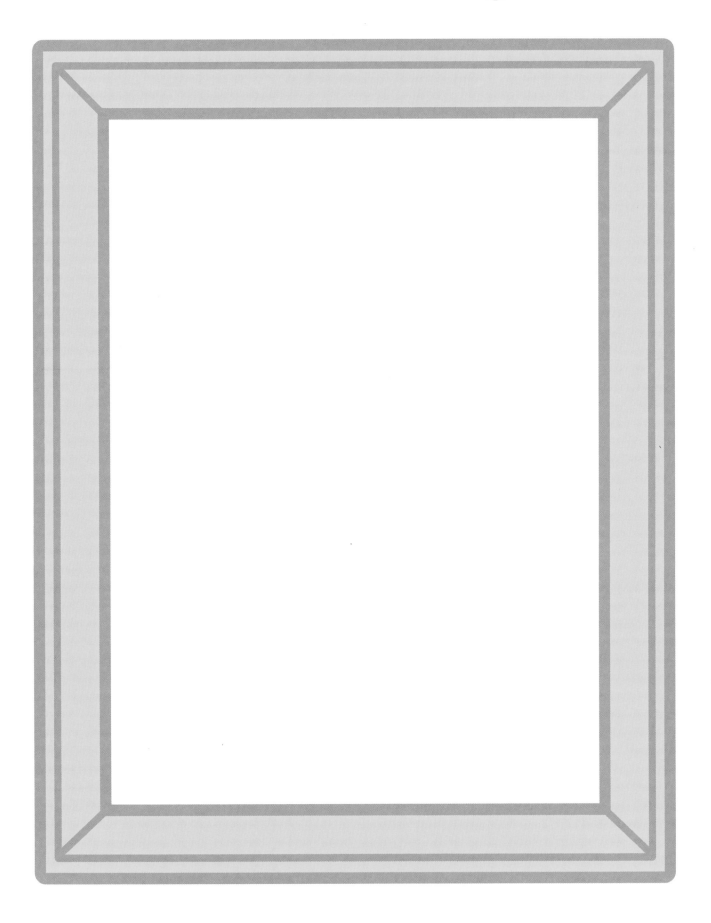

cake

Can you decorate a cake?

c_a_k_e

a **cake b**ake**s**

Draw a cake.

a __**ake** __**ake**s

snake

sn_____ _____ _____

snake on a rake

_____ake on a __ake

A sn**ake** eats a c**ake**.

skate

sk___a___t___e

sk**ate** through a **gate**

___ __**ate** through a __**ate**

plate

pl_____

cake on a plate

Can you draw a cake?

__ake on a ____ate

Draw a **pig** with a **plate**.

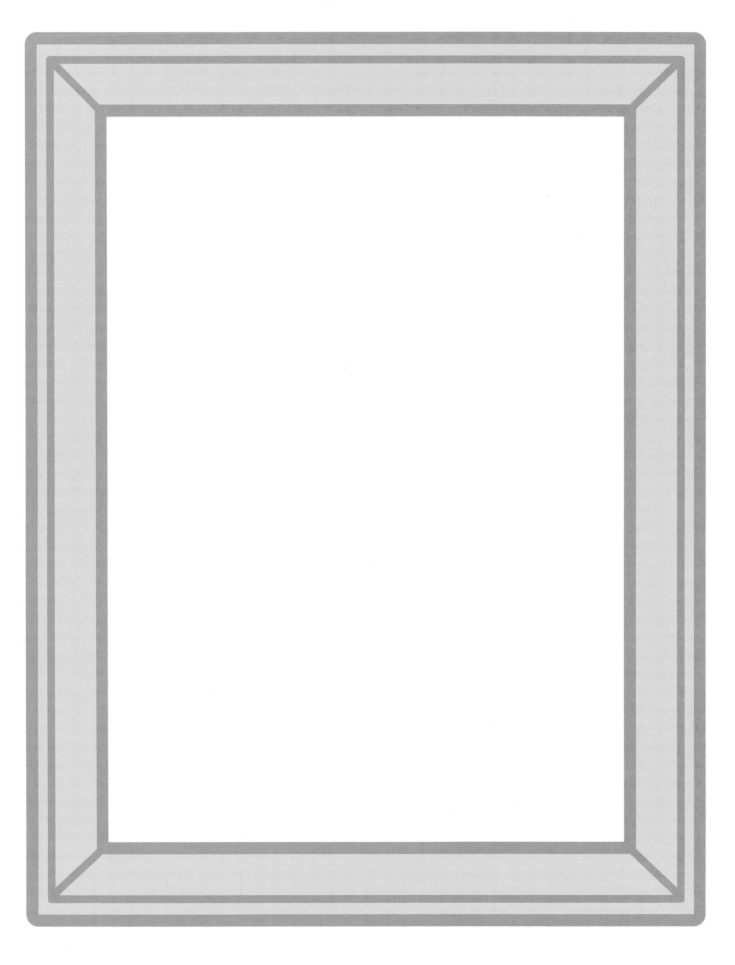

p**et**s

p _e_ _t_ s

pet net

__et __et

wet pet

_et _et

wet jet

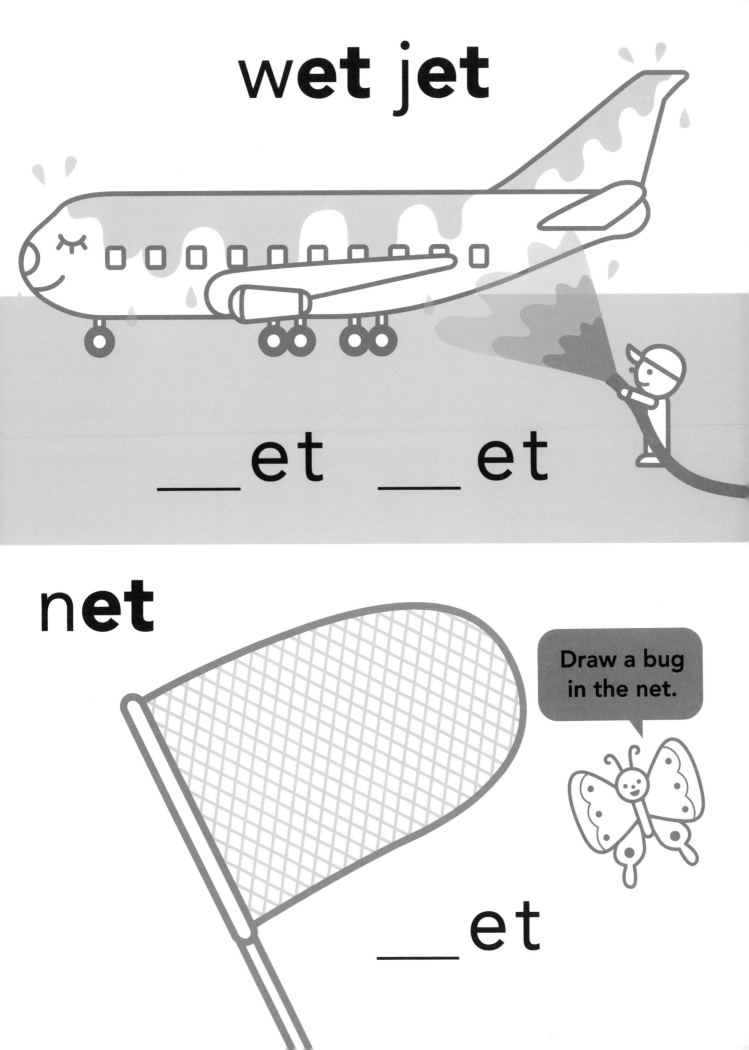

__et __et

net

__et

Draw a bug in the net.

fl**oat**

f l oat

b**oat** fl**oat**s

_**oat** ___**oat**s

goat on a boat

g_____ on a b_____

Draw a **pig** and a **bug** on a **b**oat.

ant

a_n_t_

ant in pants

ant wears __**ant**s

pl**ant**s

pl_____s

Draw a **goat** wearing p**ant**s.

p**op**

p○p

pop on top

_op on __op

cop

c___ ___

___ ___ **op**

___ **op**

___ ___ **op**

___ ___ **op**

___ ___ ___ ___ ___

___ ___ ___ ___

___ ___ ___ ___

___ ___ ___ ___ ___

Draw three animals who hop on the top!

snow

sn_o_w_

thr**ow** sn**ow**

_ _ _ _**ow** _ _ _**ow**

b**ow**

b____

_ _ _ _ **OW**

_ _ _ _

_ **OW**

_ _ _ _

_ **OW**

_ _ _

_ _ **OW**

_ _ _

Draw things that **grow**.

lamb

l___b

ram

__am

r**am** and l**amb** eat j**am**

__**am** and __**am**__
eat __**am**

I **am Sam** the **clam**.

Draw a **goat** on a **boat**.

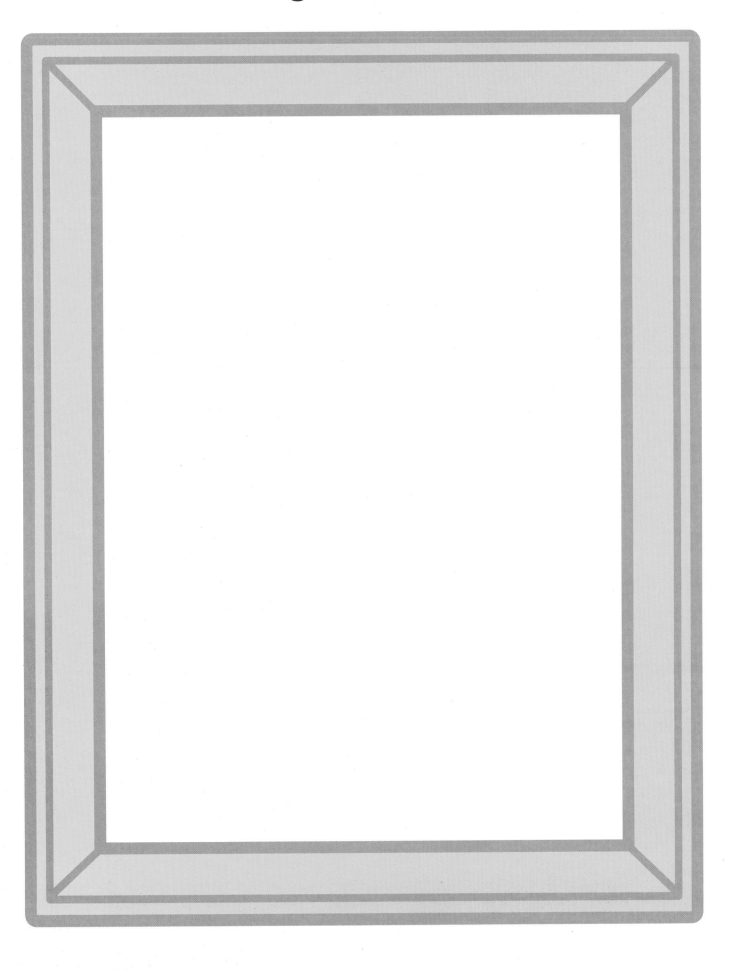

Dress me.

Word-family fun!

ig

Pretty Pig needs a wig! What **"ig"** words can you write?

pig

ug

This mug wants a hug. What **"ug"** words can you write?

mug

at

Mr. Bat has no hat! What **"at"** words can you write?

bat

ake

Jake the snake likes cake! What **"ake"** words can you write?

snake

ate

Kate loves to skate! What **"ate"** words can you write?

skate

et

Kitty is a wet pet! What **"et"** words can you write?

pet

oat

Little Goat is warm in her coat. What **"oat"** words can you write?

goat

ant

A small ant needs smaller pants. What **"ant"** words can you write?

ant

op

This cop wants you to stop! What **"op"** words can you write?

cop

ow

Do you like to throw snow? What **"ow"** words can you write?

snow

am

Sam is a happy clam. What **"am"** words can you write?

clam

MORE COLORING . .
 MORE DRAWING . . .
 MORE LEARNING . . .

MORE FUN!